Walking Under an Open Heaven

Matthew Robert Payne

Craig Beeson

To sow into Matthew's writing ministry, to request a personal prophecy or life coaching or to contact him, please visit http://personal-prophecy-today.com

Cover designed by akira007 at fiverr.com.

Edited by Lisa Thompson at www.writebylisa.com You can email Lisa at writebylisa@gmail.com

The opinions expressed by the author are not necessarily those of Revival Waves of Glory Books & Publishing.

Published by Revival Waves of Glory Books & Publishing PO Box 596| Litchfield, Illinois 62056 USA

Revival Waves of Glory Books & Publishing is committed to excellence in the publishing industry. Their website is www.revivalwavesofgloryministries.com Book design Copyright © 2017 by Revival Waves of Glory Books & Publishing. All rights reserved.

Paperback: 978-1-387-01252-7

Hardcover: 978-1-387-01253-4

Dedication

I dedicate this book to Bethany, the scribe angel that has been appointed to my life. Bethany helps inspire my books; she also helps me as I write and edit them. She is a good-natured friend to me as well. This work is largely due to her.

Acknowledgements

Father God

I want to thank you for loving me, for leading me, and for making me into the person that I am today. Thank you for your Son, my best friend.

Jesus Christ

Thank you for being my friend for all of my life. You have led me and trained me, and you have allowed me to write some encouraging books. You are a joy to me. You introduced me to your Father, and now, I am getting to know him better through the years. You are closer to me than any other person outside my mother.

Bill Vincent

I want to thank Bill Vincent, who produces my paperback books, my e-books, and my audio books. His company, Revival Waves of Glory Books & Publishing, has shown me great favor, and without you, I would be spending a lot more money to produce books. I give you my heartfelt thanks.

Lisa Thompson

I want to thank you for polishing my words and making this a better book. You take my simple language and make it more readable and understandable. I want to thank you for working on so many books with me. If you need editing services, you can contact Lisa at her website at www.writebylisa.com or directly via email at writebylisa@gmail.com

Craig Beeson

I want to thank Craig for being my friend, for helping with the stories in this book, and for helping me in many ways.

I want to thank Craig for helping me with Facebook ads to advertise my books. He blesses my ministry by managing my Facebook, Google, and SEO campaigns at no cost. If you have an already successful business and want to take it to the next level to maximize your profits, I suggest that you contact Craig at http://zuwengo.com/

The Readers

I want to thank my readers. You have motivated me to write this book.

Ministry Supporters

I want to thank all the people who have requested a prophecy from me and all those who have sown into my book-writing ministry. Without you, this book would not have been possible.

June and Bob Payne

I want to thank my mother and father for all of their love and support.

Angels and Saints

I want to thank all of the angels that have been part of my life. I want to also thank all the saints that have ministered to me. Thank you so much for loving on me.

Table of Contents

About Craig Beeson

I grew up in church, but because of my learning disabilities and speech issues, I didn't actually sit in Sunday school or in the service very often. Since I struggled, I helped out with the little kids instead. Because of that, I didn't grow up with a lot of religion in my life. I focused more on God's love and grace for people because of the challenges I faced.

I reconnected with God just a few months ago, but I've been growing at a very fast pace. I see other Christians struggle because they have too much religion in them and because they want to fit in the church.

Since I grew up with so much rejection, I don't care about fitting in. I'm just listening to God and the Holy Spirit and doing what they tell me to do. This path that I am currently on stretches me every day, but it's a lot of fun. I have many of stories to share with people, which encourages them. Some people don't want to be my friend anymore because they don't like the stories. That is okay. They're not really my friends if they don't want me to live a supernatural life anyhow.

About Matthew Robert Payne

Matthew was raised in a Baptist church and was led to the Lord at the tender age of eight. He has experienced some pain and darkness in his life, which has given him a deep compassion and love for all people.

Today, he runs a Facebook group called "Open Heavens and Intimacy with Jesus." Matthew has a commission from the Lord to train up prophets and to mentor others in the Christian faith. He does this through his Facebook posts and by writing relevant books on the Christian faith.

God has commissioned him to write at least fifty books in his life, and he spends his days writing and earning the money to self-publish. You can support him by donating money at http://personal-prophecy-today.com or by requesting any of his other services available through his ministry website.

It is Matthew's prayer that this book will bless you, and he hopes that it will lead you into a deeper and more intimate relationship with God.

A Definition of Open Heavens

I have tried to find a definition of this term to include in this book, but everything I found was too long, too complicated, and too convoluted.

When Jesus was baptized by John, the heavens opened, and I guess this is where the term came from. Since that day at John's baptism when the heavens opened, they have not shut, and through Jesus, every Christian has the right to live a supernatural life.

For me, an open heaven means that I can live a life when heaven invades it. Part of what it means to live under an open heaven is experiencing visitations from angels, saints, Jesus, and God on earth. Walking in prophecy and healing is also part of it although I don't walk in healing yet. Open heavens means walking in the atmosphere of heaven while on earth.

The line from the Lord's Prayer comes to mind, "On earth as it is in heaven."

I hope you enjoy this short little book of mine.

Chapter 1 - Visions of Jesus

Before I could see Jesus, I could sense him. I had encounters when I felt the presence of Jesus next to me and close to me. That was the very beginnings of having visions of Jesus for me.

Once, I was staying near my brother's place in Coffs Harbour, and I went down to a dark beach where Jesus and I carried on a conversation. Jesus told me to sit down there, and I asked, "What about people coming up behind me?"

He answered me with a concept from the Scripture. "I am your rear guard, so I'll protect you." I talked to him for about thirty minutes, and I was so in love with Jesus and so enraptured with him. As I was walking back, I asked Jesus where was he was, and he said he was just beyond the breakers. As I walked toward the breakers and toward the waves, the water receded about 100 feet. At first, the water was flowing in and out, but as I walked toward it, it receded nearly 100 feet at a time. This was like a sign to me. I told Jesus, "I want to meet you tonight."

He answered, "You're not going to meet me tonight, but you will meet me very soon." I share my life story in another book, *His Redeeming Love- A Memoir*, about how I met Jesus about a month later in the flesh. When Jesus told me that he was just beyond the breakers, I imagined that I could see him walking on the water. That was my first vision of Jesus, but I wasn't sure if it was actually a vision.

The following story is very graphic, so I want to warn you about it ahead of time. Once, I was fellowshipping in a church in a country town. I was up at the front, and worship was playing. I felt the presence of Jesus come into the church, and I turned around. Jesus was walking up the aisle toward the front. He told me, "I want you to really look at me today, Matthew."

Up until then, whenever I'd seen Jesus in visions, I didn't concentrate fully on the vision or press in to see the details because I was always scared of seeing Jesus in his glory. I was a very depressed and tormented individual. I felt that if I saw Jesus as others explained with bright shining robes and love pouring from his eyes, that I'd go to the nearest bridge, jump off, and commit suicide. Therefore, I was very careful when I saw Jesus in visions and wouldn't focus in on the vision.

That gives you some background as to why Jesus told me, "I want you to focus in today." I concentrated, and Jesus stood in front of the worship team. They kept playing. Jesus' face was red and full of blood. His whole garment was white down the front, but it was flecked red on the sides with red around the collar. I saw Jesus with the crown of thorns on his head.

He traveled through time in between when he was whipped and when he was crucified. I saw Jesus put in a robe just after he was whipped.

He asked me, "Are they singing about this?" He had obviously come from the cross. The song playing at the church was about Jesus' death.

I replied, "Yes they are."

Jesus turned around, and his back was sliced into shreds. The best way to explain it is when you dice meat, you actually cut strips of meat and then you put the knife sideways or diagonal, and you cut cubes of meat. That's what his back looked like—strips of meat. You could actually see through his flesh to his organs. It was horrific. I wonder if you can imagine this horrible scene, too!

Jesus turned around and asked, "Is this what they're singing about?"

I replied, "Yeah."

He wondered, "If I appeared like this, would they continue singing, or would they rush out the door?"

I agreed, "They'd rush out the door."

He asked, "Why are you the only person that can see me? They're singing to me. They're singing about this, but none of them have stopped singing. Why don't they recognize that I'm here?"

I observed, "I'm not sure, but they don't seem to know you."

He continued, "Make sure that when you worship, you're in the mood to worship and that you're fully engaged. Don't just worship for the sake of worship or out of habit. Who are they singing to?"

I told him, "They're supposed to be singing to you."

Jesus continued, "But I'm here. Why are they singing to me when I'm here? Why don't they stop and talk to me? Why don't they address me?"

I answered, "They don't know you're here."

"Exactly, they don't know I'm here. I'm in their midst, but they don't realize it."

That vision and conversation had a really profound effect on me and was one of the clearest visions that I have ever seen of Jesus.

I've seen Jesus lots of times, but this other vision of Jesus is mentioned in my book, *Visions of Heaven- Lessons Learned*. Once, I was at church and a worship song was playing. The lyrics said something like this, "I get down on my knees, and I worship you." The Holy Spirit told me that he wanted me to get on my knees the next time the chorus played.

I knelt down and then put up my hands in worship. Jesus appeared in a vision next to me, and he knelt down, also putting up his hands in the air. We sang the worship song to his Father together. About thirty seconds later, we both disappeared from the worship service and appeared in heaven. We were both at the foot of the throne, and Jesus was on his knees, singing his heart out and worshipping his Father. It was just one of the most enjoyable and beautiful scenes I've ever seen, to actually be with Jesus on his knees, fully submitted and humbly worshipping his Father in front of the throne room filled with people and angels. Here he was, the King of Kings, the Name above all Names, on his knees with his hands in the air, worshipping his Father. That was such a memorable and hard-to-forget vision of Jesus. Can you see that vision in your mind?

One of the aspects of having an open heaven in your life is having the ability to have regular visions of Jesus.

Craig's Thoughts

This is a story of my vision of Jesus. I was diagnosed with a tumor in my head, so I was going to the doctor. First, I had to take my mom with me to drop off my niece at school. The day before, we heard that my aunt and one of my mom's friends both had cancer and needed surgeries.

I asked God how I should pray for them because lately, I've been learning how to pray for people, and they are healed. I asked, "How do I pray for my aunt who is going to need surgery and for my mom's friend who was just diagnosed with breast cancer?" God told me to pray as I drove to the doctor and then again, the next day, when I went back to the doctor with my mom. The drive takes a half day there and back, which gave us a long time to pray. Two people praying together are much stronger than one person praying.

Ecclesiastes 4:12 tells us that a three-strand cord is not easily broken. We prayed in the car on the way there for my aunt, and we prayed on the way back for my mom's friend, Beverly. All of a sudden, when we were driving back, I saw Jesus, and he was crying. He was so happy, and he just said, "I'm so proud of you. Not many people will pray for people even just half an hour driving in a car. Not many people will ask us how to pray for people and then do what we tell them to do. They pray for people the way that they want to pray, but they don't ask us."

I learned how to help people by asking the Holy Spirit how I should pray for each person and to just keep praying as long as the Holy Spirit told me to pray. Sometimes I pray for thirty minutes, sometimes for a day, other times for a couple of weeks, and sometimes, it's just a one-minute prayer. I say, "You'll be healed in Jesus' Name," and they're healed. If you want to pray for people and see them healed, just ask Jesus and the Holy Spirit each time what to say and how long to pray. He'll tell you each time.

Questions to Consider:

1. Read this chapter again. Can you see the visions as I explain them?
2. Do you think that you are worthy of seeing Jesus in a vision?
3. What do you think is preventing you from seeing Jesus?
4. Have you ever considered asking the Holy Spirit how to pray?

Chapter 2 - Visions of God

John 14 promises us that if we obey the commands of Jesus that Jesus and his Father will come to us.

John 14:22-23 says, "Judas (not Iscariot) said to Him, 'Lord, how is it that You will manifest Yourself to us, and not to the world?'

"Jesus answered and said to him, "If anyone loves Me, he will keep My word; and My Father will love him, and We will come to him and make Our home with him."

I believe in Scripture and have childlike faith to believe in God's Word.

Matthew 5:8 tells us, "Blessed are the pure in heart, For they shall see God."

Because of this verse, I believe that it is totally possible for you to go to heaven and meet God. I believe that scripturally God and Jesus will come to our homes if we are open to it as John 14:23 says above. I believe that this verse means that they will come to your dinner table and sit and eat with you.

Once, I was at home, having dinner. My dining table was clear, and Jesus and his Father appeared, and they both sat down in chairs. They didn't eat; I didn't have a meal set out for them. But they sat down, and we had an ongoing conversation as I was eating dinner. It was totally amazing; it was one of the first times that I had a visit from God because I had recently read that passage and wondered if it was possible. This visitation, this encounter with God and Jesus in my house wasn't something I initiated. I didn't ask them to come to my house. But in a way, I did initiate it when I read that verse and wondered whether it was possible.

Can you see Jesus and the Father sitting at a table with me?

Another time, I was at a shopping center with a young man of God. I was telling him that God really loved and cared about him, but he doubted me. I took him through a process to open his spiritual eyes, and he was able to see a big ball of light standing next to us in the shopping center.

At that time, I didn't see God as a man. I needed some inner healing in my life. I used to see God as a ball of light, and because I saw God this way, I assumed that everyone else saw him the same way. One of the prophets in the Bible saw God as a ball of light. So God appeared as a ball of light to my friend, and my friend could hear in the spirit with his spiritual ears. God talked to him and comforted him. He started crying; he was overcome. As a Pentecostal, he was aware of the presence of God.

When God shows up, you can sometimes really feel his presence explode. My friend could spiritually sense the strong presence of God. He was aware that God was speaking to him, consoling and comforting him. The fact that God came from heaven and showed up to my friend was just what he needed to know. Sometimes, we just need to know that God loves us although it's something else when God visits us, showing up just to comfort us and share with us that he loves us.

You might be reading this and wondering if it's possible. You might wonder if God could show up in someone's house and have dinner with a person. You might wonder if he could show up just to bless a friend and share his love with that person to make a point.

I was aware at that time that I was being led by the Holy Spirit who directed me to open my friend's eyes so that he could see God. The Holy Spirit was running the whole show. Once again, I didn't cause God to turn up, but my willingness to co-labor with the Holy Spirit actually brought about the visitation.

Did you imagine that visitation?

Another time, I was with a young friend who was a prophet in training. We were at a park in my city, and I opened his spiritual eyes. I prayed with him to see in the spirit. I did this following the example of the prophet in the Bible in II Kings 6, who opened the servant's eyes to see the angelic army surrounding them.

I directed him to look at a building and up the top of these stairs, which was like an image of the throne room. It was high and lifted up. God the Father was seated on a throne in the Spirit in the center, and he was shining as brightly as the sunlight—even more brightly than the sun. On his right was Jesus, and on his left was Mary Magdalene. I instructed my young prophet friend to go up and speak to God and see what God had to say. He encountered God, and God had a message for him that truly blessed and impacted him.

Once again, the Holy Spirit directed this. He is like a director of a film or a director of a play. He orchestrates the visitations and everything that happens. When you're in tune with the Holy Spirit and led by him, you can bring people into these sorts of encounters. Once again, I have to say that I didn't orchestrate it; the Holy Spirit orchestrated it, but one of my friends was tremendously blessed. I don't think he ever forgot that encounter with God. It was a real blessing to see Mary Magdalene seated on the left-hand side of God and very interesting to see Jesus seated on the right-hand side. I knew Mary had some authority in heaven, but it was a real blessing to see her there.

These are just some of the visions of God that I've had. I've met God on earth a number of times, which is my

21

right since I'm his son. It's quite okay for a father to come and visit his son. I've encountered God in heaven multiple times, too.

Questions to Consider:

1. Go back and read each story and see if you can visualize what is happening. Look in your imagination and see if you can engage with the story. Can you see anything?
2. Do you think you are ready to meet God, or do you think you have to change in order to see him?
3. Do you think you need someone to help you open your spiritual eyes?
4. Do you think that God would like to bless you with a visit to heaven?

Chapter 3 - A Prophetic Atmosphere

When you walk under an open heaven, you might have a prophetic ability. Prophets aren't the only ones with prophetic ability. Every believer with the Holy Spirit can access the gift of prophecy. I share in a book called *Prophetic Evangelism Made Simple* how you can have the gift of prophecy and share prophetic words with strangers.

Last week, I was walking through my local shopping center, and I walked past this guy and received a word of knowledge; that is, I saw information in the spirit about him. I took a couple of steps, and the Holy Spirit told me to go back. So I went back to him, and I said, "Excuse me, I have a gift, and from time to time, that gift allows me to give a message to a person. Today, I have a message for you." He looked at me expectantly.

I continued, "You're really gifted in business, and you have a real gift in your life in that area. In Christian terms, we would say that you're anointed for business, so you'll be a real success. One thing that I'd like to share with you is that God will really bless you; he'll prosper you financially if you choose a charity and decide to give a percentage of your income to a worthy charity. Whenever you spend a percentage of your income on a charity, God will enable you to financially prosper. If you want to increase your prosperity, all you need to do is increase your giving. You don't necessarily have to give to a church to be blessed by God because God really loves you for who you are. I just thought I'd bring that encouraging message to you."

He was very thankful for the word, and I was confident that I'd said everything the Holy Spirit wanted me to say. The church was mentioned along with God, so he was pretty sure that I was a Christian because of the wording I used. A seed was planted. When you walk under an open heaven with a prophetic ability, it overshadows you.

Once, I escaped to another state when I thought my parents were going to call up psychiatrists and have me locked up. I was mentally ill and had quit taking my medication. I was afraid to be in my own house, so I called my brother, and he flew me to another city in Australia. He planned to check with my parents to see if they were after me and if they were going to try to lock me up.

A certain grace can come upon you when you're in another city. I stayed with this woman who told me, "Here is some money that your brother has given me. Go to the shopping center. I'm really busy at the moment, but come back in six hours at 2 p.m., and I'll arrange to talk to you more then. We'll spend some time together, but you need to leave now." I did as she said. As soon as I walked into the mall and saw the people, I could sense information about every single person there. I knew specific things about them, such as that the man in the last story was gifted for business.

In my book, *Prophetic Evangelism Made Simple*, I call this the 100 percent anointing. This anointing comes on your life when you're walking in this prophetic atmosphere, where you can speak to everyone you see about an issue in their life.

I walked by a veterinary facility where a woman was serving at the counter. I told her that she's really making heaven cry. "The saints of heaven and Jesus are really sad because you lost a cat and you just won't stop crying. Your cat died two weeks ago," I told her. "You keep on crying, and you're making heaven really sad. Please try and address this. Ask Jesus for help with your sadness, and see if you can buy another cat to love because you're really making heaven cry."

Everyone at the facility, the rest of the staff, stood there with their jaws dropped open in shock at this total stranger who walked in and spoke with such accuracy to their friend. They all knew that she was struggling because she was crying at work. You can make this kind of difference when Jesus gives you information about people. You simply need to obey and use the information to encourage others.

I met some young Catholic schoolgirls that day, and because I had this gift, I knew things about each one. I stopped these five girls and gave a word of knowledge to each of them. I said, "Let me see if I can tell each of you something positive about your personalities. I'll tell you one great thing about your personalities." Then, I described one positive personality attribute of each girl from the first one to the fifth one. They all agreed that I was right about each of them and were amazed at the words. Then, I told them, "I'll go back and say another positive thing from the last one to the first." I spoke over each one and was right again.

"How would you like to hear from the Holy Spirit like I do?" I asked. They replied that they were Catholics, so I lead them in a sinner's prayer so that they would know that they were saved. I then prayed for the Holy Spirit to come upon them, and they all started to glow with the glory of the Lord. I told them after the second prayer that now they could do the same thing for people if they wanted to try it. They were really encouraged and blessed that I had taken time to share with them.

When I had lunch, I was talking to a guy sitting next to me who was also eating his lunch. I used my prophetic ability and spoke to him about his life. The prophetic word had him speaking, and he admitted that he hadn't been to church for years. I was able to lead him in a prayer of repentance, and he told me that he was going to go back to church that weekend. I was very happy that the Lord used me to encourage him and bring him back to the Lord. The gift of prophecy is very handy.

Those events happened over the course of just one day. During the six hours that I spent at the mall, I spoke to five or six other people that I haven't even mentioned here. I think I spoke to about fifteen people that day and gave each of them prophetic words. I call that the 100 percent anointing.

Another time, when I had the 100 percent anointing, I exited the train in my city, Sydney, Australia. Once again, I had information about everyone that I saw. At that time, I learned that it's best to only speak to the ones that the Holy Spirit wants you to talk to, and I had learned to ask Jesus who he wanted me to speak to. I'd only address certain people that he wanted me to talk with. As I saw the needs of the others that I didn't prophesy over, I'd just pray for them.

I've since learned that I can call on my prophetic angel and ask him for his help, and if he manifests in my life, I can transition directly into the 100 percent anointing at will. This is really handy if I have someone with me and I want to teach them about prophetic evangelism. Normally, wherever I go, I'm always receiving messages for others because I'm under an open heaven and I have a prophetic gift.

Questions to Consider:

1. If everyone that is born of God can prophesy, do you think you can also receive this gift?
2. Do you think that the gift of prophecy would be helpful for you to reach out to others?
3. Why do you think God gives me the 100 percent anointing?
4. Do you think that you can receive the 100 percent anointing?

Activation prayer:

If you want the gift of prophecy so that you can prophesy over people, pray this prayer.

Dear Father,

Paul encouraged us to seek the gift of prophecy, and today, I ask for you it. I ask you for the three gifts: prophecy, word of knowledge, and word of wisdom. I ask that from today forward, these gifts will manifest in my life. I will faithfully use these new gifts as the Holy Spirit leads me.

In Jesus' Name I ask.

Further Reading:

If you prayed that prayer, I encourage you to study the gifts that you have received.

I have two books that are 99 cents on Kindle that will help you. Each book contains a prayer for you with an opportunity to prophesy over my life to practice your new gift and receive some feedback.

A Beginner's Guide to the Prophetic

Prophetic Evangelism Made Simple

Chapter 4 - Visions of Angels

Meeting angels can be exciting. I tell this story in another book of mine. One time, I was with a friend on Valentine's Day. We were having an all-nighter; we had stayed up all night. We went to a food court with a number of restaurants all together and a spacious eating area. We were there having bacon and eggs and a beautiful breakfast, and suddenly, the whole dining area filled up with angels!

I was amazed. My friend liked to talk, and he was chattering away. I interrupted, "Hold on a second; this whole dining area has just filled up with angels." My friend looked around, but he couldn't see them, so he continued talking. I very rarely do this, but I zoned out and stopped listening to him.

I asked Jesus, "Why are all the angels here?" I asked this because I have learned that when many angels turn up, they normally have a specific purpose.

Jesus answered, "It is Valentine's Day, and I love you, and I wanted to bless you." It was amazing, and I was overcome with peace and the presence of God because of the anointing of the angels.

Jesus continued, "Look on the left-hand side, by the left-hand column, on the row of chairs on the left. See the third set of chairs on the left?"

I answered, "Yeah."

He continued, "Take a look at the aisle seat. Can you see the angel sitting there?"

I replied, "Yeah."

Jesus announced, "He's one of my cupbearers."

At the time, I knew that a cupbearer was like a personal servant, a personal valet to the king. I talked to my mother afterwards, and she told me about the cupbearers. They were not only personal servants to the king, but in the days when kings could be poisoned by chefs, the cupbearer used to drink some of his wine and eat a portion of his food before the king ate so that the cupbearer would lose his life if the drink or the food was poisoned. He was similar to a bodyguard that put his life on the line, not just a personal servant. Jesus doesn't need a bodyguard any more.

You might remember that when Joseph was in prison, a cupbearer of the king was put in prison with him. This is really an official and important job, which is why the cupbearer could talk to the Pharaoh when he was released and tell him about his dream because he was close to the king and had access to him.

When I met the cupbearer, I went up and put my arm around him and told him, "I love you."

The cupbearer responded, "I love you, too." I was blessed me that this cupbearer not only knew me but loved me.

I realized at that point that this was the job that I wanted in eternity. Out of all the visions of angels, meeting Michael or the archangel Gabriel, meeting some of the four living creatures, out of all the encounters I've had with angels, this was my very favorite encounter. I loved it because the cupbearer's job is to serve Jesus coffee and put Jesus' suits out. He attends every one of his meetings and listens every time Jesus speaks. He travels everywhere with Jesus. If you can imagine, that would just be the most amazing job in the universe. I will never forget that encounter.

I had written the chapter titles for this book. I woke up yesterday and came out into my living room. The whole living room was full of my five angels, each with different jobs in my life. Each of them had manifested instead of just being in the background. I could feel their presence, and I could see them. My two sisters were there also. I have a sister, Karen, and a sister, Talitha, in heaven. Karen is a ballet dancer, and Talitha is a commercial artist. They were in the room along with Bob Jones and a couple of other saints from heaven. My whole living room was full, full of the glory. It was really encouraging to have the angels there and be talking to them and encountering them.

I was thinking about opening a Microsoft Word file and starting a conversation with everyone and recording what they said, but I had the sense that the reason why they appeared was so that I would meditate about doing this book on open heavens. I wanted to confirm that the Lord really wanted me to write this book.

I've just been working really hard, putting out a book every six weeks. I'd just finished editing a book, and I was a bit tired. I wanted to rest for a while before I actually worked on this new book. When the angels showed up with the saints, this was just an indication that I really do live under an open heaven. My house is an open access point for heaven, and I really live a supernatural life.

So the next day, which was today, I walked out, and the same thing happened—my living room was full of my angels, fully manifested and here with me now. With that encouragement two days in a row, I started this book.

I have a female angel, Bethany, which is also the name of a special town in the Bible. I was talking to her in my city, and I was walking down some steps toward my train. I saw an image in my head of one of my favorite actresses, Keira Knightley. I saw her in a movie called *Begin Again*, which was a really amazing movie about a young girl recording an album on the streets of New York. Keira Knightley looked really beautiful. When I saw the image of Keira Knightley in my mind as a vision, Bethany told me, "That's what I look like."

As I've said about the visions of Jesus, I recognize angels and saints in my house. I meet them in visions, but I don't focus in very clearly on them or look at their features. I knew that Bethany existed and that she was a female. I've talked to her and knew a bit about her personality, but I've never seen her face clearly. When she showed me the image of Keira Knightley, I came home and Googled Keira Knightley, choosing a picture to put as my computer background so that I could really focus on her.

Bethany is an angel that helps me write my books. I write according to my own spirit and her influence along with the influence of the Holy Spirit. She inspires me and works with me to come up with the subject matter, titles for books, and chapter titles. She works closely with me. She should receive much of the glory for many of my books. These are some of my visions of angels, and I hope you're encouraged.

These Two Angel Stories Are about Craig Beeson

First, I wanted to speak to my friend Craig in the U.S. about doing a Facebook ad for one of my books. However, it was the middle of the night there.

Half an hour later, he messaged me and told me that my angel had tapped him on the head and woken him up. He checked Facebook and saw my message on Facebook chat, and we talked on Skype ten minutes later.

I didn't send my angel. I just wanted to speak to my friend. God knows our heart's desires and acts accordingly on our behalf.

I was having trouble not being able to post on Facebook two days ago, and this friend prayed for my computer. I could then post on Facebook. I had not been able to post for hours.

I asked him what to do if I had the problem again, and he was asleep and unable to pray. He told me, "Just ask your angel to wake me up any time you need me."

God acted on those words of his today when I needed him.

Second, Craig shared this story.

This is about my guardian angel's nickname. I read that every angel has a name, and you can ask your angel their name. I was sitting down in my house, and I asked the Holy Spirit, "What's my angel's name?" The Holy Spirit told me that his name was CT. I saw a large black angel that was very muscular, big, and very, very strong. He had extremely broad shoulders, bigger than any body builder.

Then I asked the Holy Spirit, "What does CT stand for?" The Holy Spirit replied, "Chicken Tacos," and he burst out laughing. All of a sudden, I could see my angel glaring at the Holy Spirit because the Holy Spirit was laughing and laughing. Since that day, whenever I'm eating chicken tacos, I think about my guardian angel, and I start laughing.

Even now, as I dictate this for Matthew to include in the book, I have a breeze all around me. I had a prophetic message some time ago that spoke about this breeze on my face. The word said that I would have cool breezes from the sea, and now, I have breezes from my angel all the time. I'll be sitting around with no wind blowing and no air conditioning on. Even so, I will have a breeze moving around my body, and I know it's my angel flapping his wings and just saying hello to me, confirming that I'm doing a good job.

Questions to Consider:

1. Do you think that there is always a reason for each encounter with angels?
2. Do you think that angel's thoughts are always influencing you?

3. Did you see the cupbearer in the vision? How would you like to be Jesus' cupbearer?
4. Would your life be different if your living room were filled with angels and saints? Do you think you could experience this type of open heaven?
5. Do you think that angels will act according to your desires?
6. Do your angels do anything to let you know they are there?

Chapter 5 - Visions of Saints

I was having a lot of visions of Jesus. Once, I was in McDonald's with Jesus, talking to him. I asked, "Can you bring some guests from heaven?" People have asked me how I started encountering saints. Although I think I had encountered saints before this, my encounters really started when I intentionally asked Jesus.

He replied, "Who do you want me to bring?"

I answered, "You surprise me."

The next time Jesus showed up, he had Mary Magdalene with him. My eyes filled with tears because I knew what a close relationship Jesus and Mary Magdalene shared. Mary Magdalene started to visit me regularly, and later on, other saints began visiting me as well.

Although I'm not sure of the exact time, I think about a year ago, I was walking down the road. Every time I started to talk with Jesus, an angel, or a saint, I suddenly had feelings of guilt and shame. At that time, I had a pornography problem. As soon as the saint, Jesus, or the angel started to talk to me, I thought about the pornography. I thought, "I'm not worthy to be talking to someone who is spiritual like this."

The thought of my sin and the shame and the sadness of my addiction to pornography almost shut down the voice of the visitor. Often when I leave my house, I will have an encounter as I go to the gas station. This time, Bob Jones met me outside my door, and I was walking toward the gas station. As I thought about the pornography issue, Bob Jones told me, "Pornography is the last sin that has a hold of you. It's the last bastion of hope that the devil has in you. When you receive some inner healing, you'll be able to break free of that pornography addiction. Your pornography addiction does not define you."

Then Bob Jones went on to list twenty personality characteristics about me that he loved. He told me, "You're humble, you're kind, you're zealous, you're compassionate, you're loving, you have childlike faith, you're innocent, you're obedient, you're faithful…."

As he listed these characteristics that heaven saw in me, he continued, "When heaven looks at you, they see these characteristics. They're honestly not looking at your shortfall with your pornography problem."

Bob really helped remove the guilt and shame so that I could cope with that. He is pleased that I shared this. You can be walking under an open heaven with encounters with saints, angels, and Jesus and still struggle with sin in your life. As I edit this book now about six weeks after the initial recording, I am experiencing some freedom from that sin.

Once, I was again walking to the gas station, and I was really depressed. I also tell this story in another book of mine. Mary Magdalene and Martha showed up. Both of them had long hair down to their waists. They told me, "Stop here, Matthew," so I stopped.

On the ground in the spirit, I could see marks of chalk. Mary and Martha started to play hopscotch and jump through on one leg, on two legs, on one leg, and so forth. They jumped through the squares and ran back laughing and jumping through again. I was in the middle of this terrible depression, which was really demonic, but by the end of their antics, I was doubled over in stitches, laughing and really enjoying myself. After that, Mary and Martha walked to the gas station with me and watched me speak with the service station attendant as I was very encouraging to him. They were blessed to see me happy again.

That actual encounter pulled me out of my depression, which then left me. It was as if the glory and the presence on Mary Magdalene and her sister and the joy of the Lord that sprang up in me watching them, along with the laughter, broke off the demonic depression in my life.

Sometimes, when we're looking to discern the truth from error in visions, we need to look at the fruit that comes from the encounter. The encounter with Bob Jones gave me peace about my addiction, a peace that resulted in my healing. When I met Mary and Martha, the encounter was not only enjoyable but lifted a demonic attack off my life.

Another time, while I was at home, the whole house filled with saints. Once again, I was in the throes of depression. I was on Facebook all night talking, posting, following threads, and staying busy on the site. The saints just stayed with me all night, keeping me company. Over the course of a couple of hours, my depression left.

Once again, the glory and the presence of the saints and their supernatural ability broke the demonic depression off my life. I posted on Facebook that a whole lot of saints were in my house. Someone who was religious and who walks in unbelief said that they were familiar spirits. I responded that they were wonderful familiar spirits because I had battled with depression for weeks, and since they had been in my house, my depression had lifted. I was now full of peace and joy. I told the person that was pretty good fruit for familiar spirits.

People might mock you when you start to share that you're meeting angels, Jesus, and saints from heaven. Religious people, those stuck in wrong mind sets, who lack understanding, will mock you and say that you're being deceived and mixing with familiar spirits.

You just have to remember that Jesus and the Holy Spirit are in control. I remember the verse that says if a son asks for some bread, will the father give him a stone

(Matthew 7:9-11)? James 1:17 tells us that all good gifts come down from the Father of lights. We can remember these verses when we're walking under an open heaven and we experience the supernatural manifesting in our lives.

Questions to Consider:

1. Do you think that it is best to ask Jesus for encounters?
2. Do you think that you can have encounters without a great relationship with Jesus?
3. Is it important to assess the "fruit" from each encounter to ascertain its reliability?
4. Are you worthy to meet saints from heaven? And if so, who would you like to meet?

Chapter 6 - Accessing Heaven

I include the following story in another book, so I won't go into much detail here. My first time in heaven, I was with a counselor who told me to tell him what image I saw in my head. I responded, "I'm in heaven," and he was surprised. He took me through a vision where I met Jesus. I went into the throne room; I met the Father and had a wonderful experience. If you read my book, *My Visits to Heaven*, you can read a greater explanation of that encounter. However, that was my first encounter with heaven, so I knew these encounters were possible.

My book, *My Visits to Heaven*, shares quite a few of my encounters of heaven. If you're interested in heaven, you might enjoy reading it.

Once, I was with a Christian friend, and he was very depressed. I think I share this story in *My Visits to Heaven* as well. I told him, "Hold my hand," and he put his hand in mine.

I continued, "Imagine this. Imagine a fountain in front of you with three levels with water flowing down to the bottom of the fountain. A white lion is in the water at the bottom of the fountain, and he's walking around. He's swishing his tail, and now that you're here, he is looking at you. Can you see him looking at you?"

He answered, "Yeah."

I went on. "A white lamb is also walking around. He walks up to you. Can you see that?"

He replied, "Yeah."

I knew then that he was in heaven as he had entered a portal there. If you can see a lion, a lamb, and the base of a fountain, you could experience the same thing.

I showed my friend heaven. Just then, a couple of little children came down and led him on a tour of heaven. The children became tour guides, helping my friend experience some of heaven.

Just as I shared about the saints coming to my house or about Mary Magdalene and Martha playing hopscotch, the encounter in heaven freed him of his depression. I asked him whether his depression totally left. He told me that the encounter put him in a much better mood. He was really refreshed and thanked me for helping him to encounter heaven.

In this same book, I also talk about how I've had many encounters where I've visited my house in heaven. I've been able to see my living room there. A tapestry of a lion and a lamb with children gathered around hangs on the wall. When you approach the tapestry, the lion comes alive, and if you walk through the tapestry, you can enter a portal that takes you to a park in heaven where all the children play and enjoy themselves.

Another tapestry hangs in my living room of the woman washing Jesus' feet with her hair and anointing his feet with perfume. This woman, Mary Magdalene, was in the Pharisee's house, although her name is not mentioned. You can also go through the tapestry to a portal to Mary Magdalene's house.

For many years, I worked a job for Jesus out of obedience. As I was serving him, I promised to do another future job for Jesus that I believed I had to do. I said that I'd go through all of it if I could live in a house next to Mary Magdalene in heaven. Mary obviously lives somewhere else in heaven and is not actually my next door neighbor. However, in this tapestry in my house, you can go through the portal into Mary Magdalene's house.

My house isn't situated next to Mary's house in heaven, but I can walk through the tapestry into her home and meet with her.

As such, a portal is just a place that takes you from one place to another in an instant so that you don't have to physically travel there. You just walk through this tapestry to her house.

Recently, I gave people a choice on my website. I'll talk to you on Skype and hold your hand spiritually and take you to heaven. You can then donate to my ministry as you feel led.

Two weeks ago, I took a woman to heaven who had given me a donation. She was able to meet her mother in heaven. She then told me that she had three miscarriages, including a daughter. She met her daughter in heaven, and I was helping her ask her daughter questions and leading her through the vision and the encounter in heaven.

One of the questions she asked her daughter was what she does in heaven. Her daughter answered that she's an artist. She sculpts and paints commercial art. Her daughter showed her a picture on the wall of her house, a picture of a boat pulled up on the Sea of Galilee with Peter and the disciples. Jesus is on the beach, cooking the fish, according to the biblical account after Jesus rose from the dead. Peter was getting out of the boat. I told this woman to walk up to the painting, and it came alive. Jesus stepped out of the picture and came into the living room of the house and started to talk to her. She had a wonderful encounter with Jesus.

The daughter was really happy to see her mother and to meet her for the first time. She took the mother's hand and led her to her personal gallery with three stories of paintings. At one point, I had to go to the bathroom and fix a cup of coffee. I left the mother alone with her daughter in the vision. I came back about ten minutes later, and she had seen four of her daughter's paintings. The daughter explained each one to her.

She was able to access heaven again through this portal that I showed her. She will continue to tour her daughter's gallery, taking excursions in heaven with the young child who was her escort, a tour guide for heaven.

Craig Beeson's Stories

First, Craig had a vision of heaven and was sitting in the throne room next to God. God rose from the throne and said that my friend should sit on Jesus' throne and be in charge. According to Revelation, we are allowed to sit on Jesus' throne. God chuckled as he walked off.

Craig felt that he was not worthy, yet as God was not there, he started to command changes in sex trafficking and other terrible events on earth.

God returned and said that since man has free will, man should speak declarations over the earth. I, Matthew, am totally amazed at this story.

Next, Craig had a vision of his mansion in heaven. He shared the following.

When I was a little kid, I used to dream about a big white mansion on top of a green hill overlooking the sea. It was of Roman architecture with tall Roman columns, similar to the White House. I used to think about buying this mansion when I was older and adopting twenty kids from all over the world to live there.

I didn't really think much about why, but I thought about me and the kids and how much fun we would have. When I saw the mansion, I would look at all the fun things to do. It had lots of stuff to play with, the perfect playhouse for kids inside and outside. I also had a room full of rare gemstones, big huge gemstones, which was like my trophy room.

Recently, I paid Matthew Robert Payne to take me to heaven because I've never been there. We walked up to my mansion, and he announced, "Oh, I see a big white mansion with Roman columns and architecture."

That's when I started crying because I knew that was the same mansion that I'd imagined as a kid. God told me, "That was your mansion. As a child who had a tough life growing up, I was showing you your mansion in heaven so that you'd have hope for the future and so that you wouldn't give up."

That vision of heaven really touched me, and I was crying for a long time.

Questions to Consider:

1. Do you think you are worthy to visit heaven?
2. Where would you like to visit in heaven?
3. Do you agree that it is our right to visit heaven as believers?
4. If I showed you a portal and you were able to visit heaven, do you think you could return to heaven on your own?

Chapter 7 - Portals in my House

As I briefly shared before, a portal is a place of access where you can travel from one place to another. Instead of angels clearing a path when they come down to earth and instead of going through a long process to have an encounter in your house, a portal gives you continued and open access. It is similar to the ladder that Jacob saw, a ladder going up to heaven. A portal is simply an open access point from one place to another that saves a lot of time and effort.

I have two portals in my house. I sit at my computer, and in front of me, on my right-hand side, is my kitchen. Often, I'll be talking on Skype or working on my computer, and a saint, God, or Jesus will appear in my kitchen. They don't come from outside through my door; they don't come through my window. However, the next thing I know is that they're standing in my kitchen, so they come through a portal.

I was having a conversation with God and writing my book, *Conversations with God: Book 1.* I was dialoguing with God, typing in my conversation and then typing God's reply. God was talking to me and telling me how much he loved me. Suddenly, he came through the portal in my kitchen. I was typing God's words as he told me he loves me, and he was standing there with tears in his eyes, actually showing me how much he loved me by showing up.

It's really exciting to have a portal in your house as it means that you have an open atmosphere in your house where the spiritual realm can access and enter your house. I suppose it's like having access to a secret club. You might have a specific key or specific identification that allows you into a special club. All of the public would love to come into the club, but only the people with the special access pass can gain admittance. So it is with the portal in the house. It's a special access point where the spiritual realm can enter your home.

I was playing music by Keith Green the other day and was watching a YouTube video as he sang. As I was watching it, Keith Green appeared in my kitchen and started talking to me about the song. After the song finished, Keith began talking to me about how much he loves me and how much I've grown since I was a child when I used to listen to him. He told me that it's such a blessing to come and be part of my life and share things with me. He was able to access the portal and come straight into my home from heaven. He would have stepped out of heaven and right away, been in my house. No preparation was needed. It's as if you opened a door in one country and went through the door into another country, an open access point.

I have another portal at the end of my bed in my bedroom. About four days ago, I was in bed, having trouble sleeping. Michael, the archangel, came through the portal in my bedroom. I do a lot of talking and dialoguing with God and saints in my bedroom as I'm trying to go to sleep. Michael just showed up and had a conversation with me, and once again, he came through the portal and was standing at the end of my bed, talking to me, consoling me, and giving me something to think about so that I wouldn't focus on not being able to sleep.

If you live under an open heaven, if an open heaven is over your life, and if angels, saints, and Jesus start to visit your house regularly, then God will probably open up a portal in your house. You'll first discover the saints; if you're close to the portal, you'll see them first when they just appear in your house at that spot.

My five angels are always in my house. I suppose they go to heaven from time to time and spend time there as well, but they're always in my house. However, they are not always manifesting, and I can't always sense their presence.

Like I said before, yesterday I came out, and they were all fully manifested. I could feel their presence and see them, encounter them, and talk to them. The same was true this morning. I came out, and all the angels were here, which was confirmation that I was going to produce this book.

Some people can teach you how to open portals. I don't know how to open a portal. Although I walk in the supernatural, I don't know a lot about some aspects of the supernatural. I've never known any teachers who taught about how to open portals. However, I know that it can be done. All I know is that if you're a really close friend of Jesus and if you're really intimate with him, then he will open up portals in your house. I imagine that the number of portals you have in your home depends on how big your house is. For example, if you had an eight-bedroom house with five bathrooms, you might have five portals or entry points into your house. The number of portals will increase or decrease according to the size of your house. My portals are simply right by where I spend the majority of my time.

This is an easy way for heaven to access your house.

Questions to Consider:

1. What is a portal?
2. Do you think you would have a portal in your house if you only have occasional visits to heaven?
3. Do you think that your church might have a portal?
4. Do you think that evil spirits could enter your house through a portal?

Chapter 8 – Abundant Money Supply

A time might come when you might need an abundance of money in your life. I recognize abundance as having enough to supply your needs and having money left over to share and give to other people. I feel that a Christian might not have an abundance of money coming in if they're not prepared to give and share their money. This lack of giving, a lack of wanting to give to God, might shut the flow of supernatural giving in their life.

I spend nearly all the money that comes in through my ministry on publishing books. From time to time, the Lord will lead me to give money to other people, and I'll give money as the Holy Spirit desires.

A couple of years ago, I read that you can have a finance angel, and I talk about this angel in my books on angels. I read that if you learn his name, you can ask him to go and get your finances. I had a need for $450 to publish a book, so I sent the angel out for the money. Within a week, $550 had come in. The financial angel blessed me. I never sent him out again, but he was in my life, and from that point on, he supplied all my financials needs.

Once, I was on a Facebook live broadcast giving prophecies. Someone asked, "How do I have fruit that remains?"

I replied, "One way to have fruit that remains is to sponsor a book of mine. If you paid for the book, everyone that is blessed by the book would be fruit, and the fruit would remain whenever the book was bought. Everyone that read the book would be blessed, which would be fruit that would then turn into a spiritual reward for you."

Well, that person didn't take me up on the offer, but someone else on Facebook live asked how much it cost to sponsor a book.

I answered that it costs a minimum of $1,500 Australian for a book and that I had a book that would cost about that much coming up. He told me that he would send me a private message. In the private message, he told me that he talked to his wife, and they agreed that the Lord wanted me to have the money, and he wanted to sponsor a book. I wrote a book called *Deep Calls unto Deep*, which was a book that answered fourteen questions on the prophetic. When that book was released, I included Greg's sponsorship of the book in the acknowledgements. I have now had three people sponsor a book for me. When people give me money, it's a real blessing, and my finance angel is certainly behind it.

I started my prophetic website where I asked for a donation of $30 Australian for a prophecy. I found that more people have given my ministry money without even wanting a prophecy than the actual money I've earned from charging people for prophecies. I've found that a lot more money has come into my ministry, supplying my needs as people have given me donations without even requesting a prophecy. The Lord is aware of my needs.

Jesus knows that the books cost thousands of dollars. I just produced a book that cost $6,200 Australian, or about $5,000 US, just to edit the book. It then had to be published and a cover had to be made for it, which cost another $400. Publishing that book cost $6,600 Australian. That book was updated and then republished from one of my older books. Jesus wanted that book republished, so he brought the people to give to that need.

I received a prophecy about six weeks ago that said, "You have not because you ask not." The word continued, "God wants to give to you, but you need to ask him for finances." So I considered that prophecy as a word of wisdom, a directional word.

I took hold of the prophecy, and I asked Jesus for $500 Australian, and the next day, someone donated that exact amount as a gift to me. I asked Jesus for another $500 Australian, and someone donated $720. I then asked for another $500, and within a couple of days, someone donated $1,280. I asked for $1,000, and within a week and a half, someone again gave me that exact amount. All this money came in as I needed the $6,600 for the book that I was updating and publishing.

You might wonder why some of the funds came in a week and a half instead of a day. I was waiting for a friend as I had promised to donate some money to her. I told her that I would bless her with some money when she set up a PayPal account. She needed money to move out of a women's hostel and into her own apartment. This was going to cost $680 Australian or $500 US. Once I released that $680 Australian to her, an hour later, $1,000 Australian came in. One of the keys to abundance is to be open to the Holy Spirit and to give money when the Holy Spirit guides you to give money.

The finances needed to transcribe, edit, and publish this book are already in my PayPal account. The money I need for each book seems to come to me just when I need it. I never seem to have to wait for a week or two for the finances to publish a book. The money that I need for each book seems to come in right when I need it. This is a testimony of the fact that my financial angel is hard at work.

Another key to all of this that I feel is important is that all of my books are priced at 99 cents on Kindle when I could charge $3 to $5 for most of my books, especially the longer ones. This book is small, so 99 cents is reasonable. I've never published a book that was this short. One of the keys is that I'm not trying to make money from my books or off people; I'm doing God's will. I am pretty sure that when people read my books and love them, they are impressed with how inexpensive they are. These people realize that my book publishing is a ministry and that I am not out to make money off people, so they freely give to me.

It is very rewarding to be supported by God and angels in all that I do.

Questions to Consider:

1. What do you think is a key to receiving from God?
2. Do you think that the more you are prepared to give, the more God gives to you?
3. Do you think you need to be in ministry to prosper in finances?
4. Do you think that you need to change anything in your life to start to prosper?

Chapter 9 - Open Heaven in my House

My house has an open heaven in it. I've found that people who have visited my house are blessed by the peace that resides there; it has a lot of peace. You'll remember that when Jesus sent out his disciples without any money, and they went out to minister, he told them, "And if the house be worthy, let your peace come upon it: but if it be not worthy, let your peace return to you" (Matthew 10:13 – KJV). So the peace of God and his presence travels with people. I have the peace and presence of God in my house. As I've shared, my house has portals in it and is an open access point from heaven.

I had a friend from Papua New Guinea come and stay with me while he attended a conference. The first night, saints were visiting the house that wanted to talk with him. He was having encounters with saints.

Moses and David both came, and Moses gave him a staff, and David gave him a sling. Ian was really blessed by the open heaven in my house; it was as if he came into an environment that was charged with heaven. He had no doubt that when he finished his stay in my house that God was with me and that I was a really special person. I not only have a house with an open heaven, but I myself am an open heaven. No matter where I go, wherever I access, saints, angels, and Jesus will visit me. I carry this open heaven around with me. I can introduce people to saints, to Jesus, and to angels no matter where I am.

I can even introduce people to saints, angels, and Jesus over the internet and Skype. I can have a Skype meeting with you, and you can meet saints, angels, and Jesus in your own house. I can help you step into that vision. Of course, I'd ask you for a donation for my time, but I'm happy to do that.

Ian told me that he felt the peace in the house. He also encountered saints in my house and was able to talk to them even when I had gone to bed. He didn't need me there to talk and dialogue with them.

I have five angels in my life: the finance angel; a prophetic angel or my guardian angel; Elijah, who is a CEO angel; Bethany, a scribe angel; and Jonathan, a big, imposing angel of protection. Other angels will often manifest in my house as well.

Special angels sometimes manifest in my home. Michael, Gabriel, and other important angels have been to my house. I've seen the four living creatures; the ox of the four living creatures came to my house the other day. Saints from heaven are always coming through portals in my house and interacting with me.

Most of the time, the saints come to my house after heaven initiates the visits. In other words, most of the time, I don't request that a saint actually come to my house. I don't say, "I want to see Mary Magdalene," and she appears in my house. Most of the time, heaven, the Holy Spirit, and Jesus orchestrate the saint's visit to my house. They know that the saint has a special message or something special to impart into my life at that time.

Like I already shared in the book, I was visited by a whole roomful of saints who didn't really talk to me. They just sat in my living room while I was on Facebook, and my depression lifted. I also shared about the time I was depressed when Mary and Martha skipped and played hopscotch, bringing me out of my depression.

God has a reason for everything, and God is the God of reason beyond our understanding. I feel that if we move into arenas where we are requesting meetings with saints, we might be on dangerous ground where the saints could become idols to us and even more important than Jesus. I tend to personally leave the visitations to heaven most of the time so that heaven orchestrates the visitations and encounters that I have.

I have sometimes been told by Jesus that I can request any saint to come to earth to dialogue with. The Holy Spirit is very aware that I have a need. If I ask to speak to Elijah, I have a real reason why I want to talk to him. Perhaps I want to talk to him about the state of the church, or I need help with a blog or Facebook post to officially warn the church. I might be making an official eye-opening statement to the church, and I want him to manifest his mantle and his anointing into the actual writing of the piece.

When you have a relationship with Jesus and an open heaven over your life, then you can reach a point where you can personally request to meet angels and saints. I could ask all of my angels to manifest, and they could all appear and start to talk to me. They are in the background most of the time, and I know they're here, but I don't actually sense their presence.

From time to time, I could ask them to manifest, but just like yesterday and today, Jesus had a reason for them to show up. He had a reason to encourage me to finish taking a break from working on books so that I would be motivated to finish the voice files that will become the book that you're reading. I have now completed the nine chapters that I had planned, but I've decided to add one more chapter, which you're probably waiting for. That chapter is called "Keys to an Open Heaven."

Questions to Consider:

1. Do you think it is possible for you to walk under an open heaven?
2. Do you think your open heaven would travel with you?

3. Do you think that you should pursue encounters with saints and angels, or should you let heaven initiate the encounters for you?

4. Do you think you are reading this book by coincidence, or do you think you are reading this because God is going to open heaven over your life?

Chapter 10 - Seven Keys to an Open Heaven

Key 1 - You Have to Believe It Is Possible

First of all, you have to believe that you have the right to have encounters with Jesus, with angels, and with saints. You have to believe that it is possible to have these experiences. You need to believe that:

- You are worthy
- You are good enough
- You are perfect enough and
- An open heaven could appear over your life.

Jesus responds to faith, so I've written this book in order to show you what some of the aspects of an open heaven look like. Hopefully, as you've read this book, you've come to realize that it is possible. Hopefully, this book has sparked a holy jealousy in you, which is a sanctified jealousy; it's a desire to have what I have. I hope that these encounters, these descriptions of my life and different aspects of an open heaven, have helped you come to believe that it's possible.

You know that I shared about my pornography problem when I talked to Bob Jones walking down the street. As I prepare this book for publication, it's no longer an issue for me. You don't have to be perfect to have an open heaven in your life, so I hope that this book clears up any misconceptions that you might have had. Perhaps you might think that you need to be perfect, but I'm by no means perfect, either, and Bob Jones cleared up that misconception for me. I still have sin in my life. I still react sometimes when people write bad reviews, and sometimes, I argue with others on Facebook, so I'm by no means perfect.

Key 2 - Intimacy with Jesus

An intimate relationship with Jesus is of paramount importance. I think that someone could have encounters with Jesus, with angels, and with saints without having an intimate relationship with Jesus, but they might not happen much. Jesus is smart, all-wise, and all-knowing, and he might know that it could take a couple of encounters with the supernatural to spur someone on and encourage that person to become intimate with him.

In his wisdom, he might allow someone to have encounters in their life before they have an intimate relationship with him, but I really feel that one of the things that qualifies me to have an open heaven in my life is my intimacy with Jesus. There are no short-cuts to intimacy with Jesus. For more on this vital subject, see my book *7 Keys to Intimacy with Jesus*.

Key 3 - Jesus Has to Be #1 in your Life

Nothing else can be number one in your life—not your church, your money, your possessions, or anything else. Jesus must be your number one priority in life. If Jesus isn't number one in your life, if you just have a casual, average Christian's relationship with him, then angels might start to appear to you, and you might become infatuated with them and really start to have an unhealthy relationship with them.

If angels started appearing to you, you might have a relationship where they are more special and more important to you than Jesus. Jesus would not allow you to have encounters with angels so that you become closer to the angels than to him. Jesus has to be number one.

No saint in heaven can replace my love for Jesus. No matter how many times I have met Mary Magdalene, and I have met her over 100 times, she hasn't become closer to me than Jesus. Jesus is my number one and my most important friend. He is the reason for my breath. Without Jesus, I'd have no purpose for living. He has to be number one.

Key 4 - Childlike Faith

You need to believe the promises of God and that God is a good God. You've got to believe that God gives good and perfect gifts, like James 1:17 tells us. You have to have the faith not to think that you will be deceived by familiar spirits or that demons will manifest to you instead of angels. You have to believe that an angel of light will not deceive you.

I would recommend that you don't even enter this realm if you do not have childlike faith. Jesus responds to faith; the whole kingdom of God responds to faith, and you need to have this innocent faith about you. Otherwise, you will always worry about deception.

Key 5 - Faithfulness

God tests us. He gives us things to do, including projects and assignments. One of the keys to the abundant resources that I have is my obedience. Once, I was told by the Holy Spirit to give someone $1,500. I gave her the money. Another time, I was told to give $680. I gave the money, and as I shared, I received $1,000 back an hour later. You have to be faithful. You have to be proven faithful to God.

Key 6 - Obedience

You have to obey the Holy Spirit when he directs you to act. Producing this book is a work of obedience. When I was inspired by the Holy Spirit to write this book, I began to write. I was inspired by Bethany with the chapter titles, and then I took the time to record the voice recordings, edit the transcripts, and work with my editor to prepare the book.

Obedience is a key to many things in the Kingdom of God. We all know that Jesus, along with the apostles, was obedient.

Key 7 - You Have to Have a Love for It

You have to have a love for:

- Angels
- Saints
- Heaven
- Jesus
- This lifestyle
- The prophetic
- The Christian faith
- Sharing your faith
- Sharing your testimonies and
- Encouraging other people.

These are the seven keys to an open heaven. God bless.

A Prayer of Impartation

It would make little sense for me to write all about open heavens without praying for you. So I am going to pray that you have an open heaven over your life.

Dear Father,

The open heaven that I am under has come with time and experience as I have cooperated with heaven and your will. I pray that you would start to open the heavens over the lives of the readers. I pray that you would open their spiritual eyes and let them start to encounter all that heaven has for them. I pray for every reader, who has the keys that I mentioned in the last chapter, to eventually walk with encounters as great as mine or even greater. I pray that you would lead them to books on how to see in the spirit and that they might have great success in this area.

I ask this with faith in Jesus' Name, combining my faith with the readers.

Closing Thoughts

I hope that the stories and accounts in this book have stirred your spirit and that they have you excited to experience your own encounters. I live a very exciting life, and every single day, I have an encounter with heaven. It is my prayer that you will have the discipline to grow in this and become as proficient in dealing with heaven as I am.

Even when your spiritual eyes are opened, developing spiritual sight takes a lot of practice so that you can see visions clearly. Like anything worthwhile, practice is essential to developing this gift. Therefore, it is my prayer that you will endure and press through when things seem to be difficult for you.

I can share with you that it is really exciting to connect with saints, angels, and Jesus every day in my life. I pray that you will also walk in this one day.

I'd love to hear from you

One of the ways that you can bless me as a writer is by writing an honest and candid review of my book on Amazon. I always read the reviews of my books, and I would love to hear what you have to say about this one.

Before I buy a book, I read the reviews first. You can make an informed decision about a book when you have read enough honest reviews from readers. One way to help me sell this book and to give me positive feedback is by writing a review for me. It doesn't cost you a thing but helps me and the future readers of this book enormously.

If you would like to sow money into my book-writing ministry and would like to sow a portion into a book, please visit my website and ask me what projects I am working on.

To read my blog, request a life-coaching session, request your own personal prophecy, request a visit to heaven, or to receive a personal message from your angel, you can also visit my website at http://personal-prophecy-today.com All of the funds raised through my ministry website will go toward the books that I write and self-publish. Feel free to sow money into my book-publishing ministry as the Holy Spirit leads you.

To write to me about this book or to share any other

thoughts, please feel free to contact me at my personal email address at survivors.sanctuary@gmail.com

You can also friend request me on Facebook at Matthew Robert Payne. Please send me a message if we have no friends in common as a lot of scammers now send me friend requests.

You can also do me a huge favor and share this book on Facebook as a recommended book to read. This will help me and other readers.

Other Books by Matthew Robert Payne

The Prophetic Supernatural Experience

Prophetic Evangelism Made Simple

Your Identity in Christ

His Redeeming Love- A Memoir

Writing and Self-Publishing Christian Nonfiction

Coping with your Pain and Suffering

Living for Eternity

Jesus Speaking Today

Great Cloud of Witnesses Speak

My Radical Encounters with Angels

Finding Intimacy with Jesus Made Simple

My Radical Encounters with Angels- Book Two

A Beginner's Guide to the Prophetic

Michael Jackson Speaks from Heaven

7 Keys to Intimacy with Jesus

Conversations with God: Book 1

Optimistic Visions of Revelation

Conversations with God: Book 2

Finding Your Purpose in Christ

Influencing your World for Christ: Practical Everyday Evangelism

Deep Calls unto Deep: Answering Questions on the Prophetic

My Visits to the Galactic Council of Heaven

The Parables of Jesus Made Simple: Updated and Expanded Edition

Great Cloud of Witnesses Speak: Old and New

You can find my published books on my Amazon author page here: http://tinyurl.com/jq3h893

Upcoming Books

A Message from my Angel: Book 1

Lightning Source UK Ltd.
Milton Keynes UK
UKHW010048170223
417092UK00013B/716/J